50 Young Chef Recipes for Home

By: Kelly Johnson

Table of Contents

- Mini Pizzas
- Fruit Salad
- Peanut Butter Banana Toast
- DIY Tacos
- Cheesy Quesadillas
- Pasta with Marinara Sauce
- Rainbow Veggie Wraps
- Yogurt Parfaits
- Chocolate-Dipped Fruit
- Homemade Trail Mix
- Egg Muffins
- No-Bake Energy Bites
- Veggie Fried Rice
- Mini Pancakes
- Oven-Baked Chicken Nuggets
- Caprese Skewers
- Baked Potatoes with Toppings
- Grilled Cheese Sandwich
- Smoothie Bowls
- Chocolate Chip Cookies
- Apple Nachos
- Veggie Stir-Fry
- Muffin Tin Omelets
- Rice Krispie Treats
- Stuffed Peppers
- Homemade Pizza Rolls
- Savory Muffins
- Fruit Smoothies
- Pasta Salad
- Baked Zucchini Fries
- S'mores Treats
- Chicken Fajitas
- Cucumber Sandwiches
- Homemade Hummus
- Pasta Primavera
- Cheese and Crackers Platter
- Mini Meatballs
- Vegetable Soup
- Baked Apple Crisp

- Peanut Butter Cookies
- Taco Salad
- Chocolate Mug Cake
- Egg Salad Sandwiches
- Oven-Baked Fish Sticks
- Fruit and Yogurt Cups
- Zucchini Noodles
- Homemade Salsa
- Pasta with Pesto
- Mini Quiches
- Frozen Yogurt Bark

Mini Pizzas

Ingredients

- 1 package of English muffins or pita bread
- 1 cup marinara sauce
- 1 cup shredded mozzarella cheese
- Toppings of your choice (pepperoni, vegetables, etc.)
  Instructions
1. **Preheat Oven:** Preheat your oven to 400°F (200°C).
2. **Prepare Base:** Split English muffins or pita bread in half and place on a baking sheet.
3. **Add Sauce:** Spread marinara sauce over each half.
4. **Top with Cheese:** Sprinkle mozzarella cheese on top and add your favorite toppings.
5. **Bake:** Bake for about 10-12 minutes, or until cheese is melted and bubbly.
6. **Serve:** Enjoy warm!

Fruit Salad

Ingredients

- 2 cups strawberries, hulled and sliced
- 2 cups pineapple, diced
- 2 cups grapes, halved
- 2 cups kiwi, peeled and sliced
- Juice of 1 lime
- 1 tablespoon honey (optional)

Instructions

1. **Combine Fruit:** In a large bowl, combine all the fruit.
2. **Dress Salad:** Drizzle with lime juice and honey, if using.
3. **Toss:** Gently toss to combine.
4. **Serve:** Enjoy immediately or chill for 30 minutes!

Peanut Butter Banana Toast

Ingredients

- 4 slices of whole grain bread
- ½ cup peanut butter
- 2 bananas, sliced
- Honey or cinnamon (optional)

Instructions

1. **Toast Bread:** Toast the slices of bread until golden.
2. **Spread Peanut Butter:** Spread peanut butter evenly over each slice.
3. **Add Bananas:** Top with banana slices.
4. **Drizzle (optional):** Drizzle with honey or sprinkle with cinnamon if desired.
5. **Serve:** Enjoy immediately!

DIY Tacos

Ingredients

- 8 small tortillas (corn or flour)
- 1 lb ground beef or turkey (or beans for a vegetarian option)
- 1 packet taco seasoning
- Toppings: lettuce, tomato, cheese, sour cream, salsa

Instructions

1. **Cook Meat:** In a skillet, cook the ground meat until browned. Drain excess fat.
2. **Add Seasoning:** Stir in taco seasoning and follow package instructions.
3. **Warm Tortillas:** Heat tortillas in a dry skillet or microwave.
4. **Assemble Tacos:** Fill each tortilla with seasoned meat and desired toppings.
5. **Serve:** Enjoy immediately!

Cheesy Quesadillas

Ingredients

- 4 large flour tortillas
- 2 cups shredded cheese (cheddar, Monterey Jack, or a mix)
- Optional fillings: cooked chicken, beans, veggies
- Olive oil or cooking spray

Instructions

1. **Preheat Skillet:** Heat a large skillet over medium heat.
2. **Assemble Quesadillas:** On half of each tortilla, sprinkle cheese and any optional fillings. Fold the tortilla over.
3. **Cook Quesadillas:** Lightly oil the skillet and cook each quesadilla for about 3-4 minutes per side, or until golden and cheese is melted.
4. **Slice and Serve:** Cut into wedges and enjoy with salsa or sour cream!

Pasta with Marinara Sauce

Ingredients

- 8 oz pasta of your choice
- 2 cups marinara sauce
- 1 tablespoon olive oil
- Grated Parmesan cheese (optional)

Instructions

1. **Cook Pasta:** Cook pasta according to package instructions; drain.
2. **Heat Sauce:** In a saucepan, heat marinara sauce over medium heat until warmed through.
3. **Combine:** Toss cooked pasta with marinara sauce and olive oil.
4. **Serve:** Top with grated Parmesan cheese if desired. Enjoy!

Rainbow Veggie Wraps

Ingredients

- 4 large tortillas or wraps
- 1 cup hummus or cream cheese
- 1 cup shredded carrots
- 1 cup bell peppers, sliced
- 1 cup cucumber, sliced
- 1 cup spinach or mixed greens

Instructions

1. **Spread Filling:** Spread hummus or cream cheese evenly on each tortilla.
2. **Layer Veggies:** Layer carrots, bell peppers, cucumber, and spinach on top.
3. **Roll Up:** Roll the tortilla tightly, then slice in half.
4. **Serve:** Enjoy fresh or wrap in foil for later!

Yogurt Parfaits

Ingredients

- 2 cups yogurt (Greek or regular)
- 1 cup granola
- 2 cups mixed berries (strawberries, blueberries, raspberries)
- Honey or maple syrup (optional)

Instructions

1. **Layer Ingredients:** In a glass or bowl, layer yogurt, granola, and mixed berries.
2. **Repeat Layers:** Repeat layers until ingredients are used up.
3. **Drizzle (optional):** Drizzle with honey or maple syrup if desired.
4. **Serve:** Enjoy immediately!

Chocolate-Dipped Fruit

Ingredients

- 2 cups of fresh fruit (strawberries, banana slices, apple wedges, etc.)
- 1 cup chocolate chips (dark, milk, or white)
- 1 tablespoon coconut oil (optional)

Instructions

1. **Melt Chocolate:** In a microwave-safe bowl, combine chocolate chips and coconut oil. Microwave in 30-second intervals, stirring until smooth.
2. **Dip Fruit:** Dip each piece of fruit into the melted chocolate, allowing excess to drip off.
3. **Chill:** Place dipped fruit on a parchment-lined baking sheet and refrigerate until chocolate is set (about 30 minutes).
4. **Serve:** Enjoy as a sweet treat!

Homemade Trail Mix

Ingredients

- 1 cup nuts (almonds, walnuts, cashews)
- 1 cup dried fruit (raisins, cranberries, apricots)
- ½ cup chocolate chips or M&Ms
- ½ cup seeds (pumpkin seeds or sunflower seeds)
- Optional: ½ teaspoon cinnamon or coconut flakes

  ### Instructions
1. **Combine Ingredients:** In a large bowl, mix all ingredients together.
2. **Store:** Transfer to an airtight container for storage.
3. **Serve:** Enjoy as a snack on-the-go!

Egg Muffins

Ingredients

- 6 large eggs
- ½ cup milk
- 1 cup diced vegetables (bell peppers, spinach, onions)
- ½ cup shredded cheese
- Salt and pepper to taste

Instructions

1. **Preheat Oven:** Preheat your oven to 350°F (175°C).
2. **Mix Ingredients:** In a bowl, whisk together eggs, milk, salt, and pepper. Stir in vegetables and cheese.
3. **Pour into Muffin Tin:** Grease a muffin tin and pour the egg mixture evenly into each cup.
4. **Bake:** Bake for 20-25 minutes, or until set and lightly golden.
5. **Serve:** Let cool slightly before removing from the tin. Enjoy!

No-Bake Energy Bites

Ingredients

- 1 cup rolled oats
- ½ cup peanut butter
- ½ cup honey
- ½ cup chocolate chips
- ¼ cup flaxseed (optional)
- 1 teaspoon vanilla extract

Instructions

1. **Mix Ingredients:** In a bowl, combine all ingredients and mix until well combined.
2. **Chill:** Refrigerate the mixture for about 30 minutes to firm up.
3. **Form Bites:** Once chilled, roll into small balls (about 1 inch in diameter).
4. **Store:** Keep in an airtight container in the fridge. Enjoy as a snack!

Veggie Fried Rice

Ingredients

- 3 cups cooked rice (preferably day-old)
- 1 cup mixed vegetables (carrots, peas, bell peppers)
- 2 eggs, beaten
- 2 tablespoons soy sauce
- 1 tablespoon sesame oil
- 2 green onions, sliced

Instructions

1. **Heat Oil:** In a large skillet or wok, heat sesame oil over medium heat.
2. **Cook Eggs:** Add beaten eggs and scramble until fully cooked. Remove and set aside.
3. **Stir-Fry Vegetables:** In the same pan, add mixed vegetables and stir-fry for 3-4 minutes.
4. **Add Rice and Sauce:** Add cooked rice and soy sauce, mixing well. Stir in cooked eggs and green onions.
5. **Serve:** Enjoy hot!

Mini Pancakes

Ingredients

- 1 cup pancake mix
- ¾ cup milk
- 1 egg
- 1 tablespoon sugar (optional)
- Butter or oil for cooking

Instructions

1. **Mix Batter:** In a bowl, combine pancake mix, milk, egg, and sugar until smooth.
2. **Preheat Skillet:** Heat a non-stick skillet over medium heat and lightly grease with butter or oil.
3. **Cook Pancakes:** Pour small amounts of batter onto the skillet (about 2 tablespoons each). Cook until bubbles form on the surface, then flip and cook until golden brown.
4. **Serve:** Stack mini pancakes and serve with syrup, fruit, or toppings of your choice!

Oven-Baked Chicken Nuggets

Ingredients

- 1 lb chicken breast, cut into bite-sized pieces
- 1 cup breadcrumbs
- ½ cup grated Parmesan cheese
- 1 teaspoon garlic powder
- 1 teaspoon paprika
- Salt and pepper to taste
- 1 egg, beaten

Instructions

1. **Preheat Oven:** Preheat your oven to 400°F (200°C).
2. **Prepare Coating:** In a bowl, combine breadcrumbs, Parmesan, garlic powder, paprika, salt, and pepper.
3. **Coat Chicken:** Dip chicken pieces in beaten egg, then coat with breadcrumb mixture.
4. **Bake:** Place on a baking sheet lined with parchment paper and bake for 15-20 minutes, or until golden and cooked through.
5. **Serve:** Enjoy with your favorite dipping sauce!

Caprese Skewers

Ingredients

- 1 pint cherry tomatoes
- 8 oz fresh mozzarella balls
- Fresh basil leaves
- Balsamic glaze (optional)
- Salt and pepper to taste

Instructions

1. **Assemble Skewers:** On small skewers or toothpicks, alternate threading cherry tomatoes, mozzarella balls, and basil leaves.
2. **Drizzle:** Arrange on a serving platter and drizzle with balsamic glaze if desired.
3. **Season:** Sprinkle with salt and pepper to taste.
4. **Serve:** Enjoy as a fresh appetizer or snack!

Baked Potatoes with Toppings

Ingredients

- 4 large russet potatoes
- ½ cup sour cream
- 1 cup shredded cheese (cheddar or your choice)
- ½ cup cooked bacon bits (optional)
- ¼ cup green onions, sliced
- Salt and pepper to taste

Instructions

1. **Preheat Oven:** Preheat your oven to 400°F (200°C).
2. **Prepare Potatoes:** Scrub potatoes and poke several holes in each with a fork. Rub with olive oil and salt.
3. **Bake:** Place directly on the oven rack and bake for about 45-60 minutes, or until tender.
4. **Add Toppings:** Cut potatoes open and fluff with a fork. Top with sour cream, cheese, bacon bits, green onions, salt, and pepper.
5. **Serve:** Enjoy hot!

Grilled Cheese Sandwich

Ingredients

- 4 slices of bread (your choice)
- 2 tablespoons butter
- 4 slices of cheese (cheddar, American, or your favorite)

Instructions

1. **Butter Bread:** Spread butter on one side of each slice of bread.
2. **Assemble Sandwich:** Place cheese between two slices, buttered side out.
3. **Grill:** Heat a skillet over medium heat and cook the sandwich for 3-4 minutes on each side, until golden brown and cheese is melted.
4. **Serve:** Slice in half and enjoy warm!

Smoothie Bowls

Ingredients

- 1 cup frozen fruit (berries, banana, or mango)
- ½ cup yogurt (Greek or regular)
- ½ cup milk or juice
- Toppings: granola, fresh fruit, nuts, seeds, coconut flakes

Instructions

1. **Blend Base:** In a blender, combine frozen fruit, yogurt, and milk or juice until smooth.
2. **Pour:** Pour the smoothie into a bowl.
3. **Add Toppings:** Top with granola, fresh fruit, nuts, seeds, and coconut flakes as desired.
4. **Serve:** Enjoy immediately with a spoon!

Chocolate Chip Cookies

Ingredients

- 1 cup butter, softened
- ¾ cup brown sugar
- ¾ cup granulated sugar
- 1 teaspoon vanilla extract
- 2 large eggs
- 2 ¼ cups all-purpose flour
- 1 teaspoon baking soda
- ½ teaspoon salt
- 2 cups chocolate chips

Instructions

1. **Preheat Oven:** Preheat your oven to 350°F (175°C).
2. **Cream Butter and Sugars:** In a large bowl, cream together butter, brown sugar, granulated sugar, and vanilla until smooth.
3. **Add Eggs:** Beat in eggs one at a time.
4. **Mix Dry Ingredients:** In another bowl, combine flour, baking soda, and salt. Gradually add to the wet mixture. Stir in chocolate chips.
5. **Drop Cookies:** Drop rounded tablespoons of dough onto a baking sheet.
6. **Bake:** Bake for 10-12 minutes, or until edges are golden.
7. **Serve:** Let cool and enjoy!

Apple Nachos

Ingredients

- 2 large apples, sliced
- ¼ cup peanut butter or almond butter
- ¼ cup chocolate chips
- ¼ cup granola
- Optional toppings: dried fruit, coconut flakes, nuts

Instructions

1. **Arrange Apples:** Lay apple slices on a plate in a single layer.
2. **Drizzle Peanut Butter:** Drizzle peanut butter over the apple slices.
3. **Add Toppings:** Sprinkle with chocolate chips, granola, and any additional toppings.
4. **Serve:** Enjoy immediately!

Veggie Stir-Fry

Ingredients

- 2 cups mixed vegetables (bell peppers, broccoli, carrots, snap peas)
- 2 tablespoons soy sauce
- 1 tablespoon olive oil
- 2 cloves garlic, minced
- 1 teaspoon ginger, grated (optional)
- Cooked rice or noodles for serving

Instructions

1. **Heat Oil:** In a large skillet or wok, heat olive oil over medium-high heat.
2. **Add Vegetables:** Add mixed vegetables and stir-fry for about 5-7 minutes until tender-crisp.
3. **Add Flavorings:** Stir in garlic, ginger, and soy sauce, cooking for another 2 minutes.
4. **Serve:** Serve over rice or noodles. Enjoy!

Muffin Tin Omelets

Ingredients

- 6 large eggs
- ½ cup milk
- 1 cup diced vegetables (spinach, bell peppers, onions)
- ½ cup shredded cheese
- Salt and pepper to taste

Instructions

1. **Preheat Oven:** Preheat your oven to 350°F (175°C).
2. **Whisk Eggs:** In a bowl, whisk together eggs, milk, salt, and pepper.
3. **Prepare Muffin Tin:** Grease a muffin tin and distribute diced vegetables and cheese evenly among the cups.
4. **Pour Egg Mixture:** Pour the egg mixture over the vegetables and cheese until just full.
5. **Bake:** Bake for 18-20 minutes, or until set.
6. **Serve:** Let cool slightly before removing from the tin. Enjoy!

Rice Krispie Treats

Ingredients

- 3 tablespoons butter
- 1 package (10 oz) marshmallows
- 6 cups Rice Krispies cereal

Instructions

1. **Melt Butter and Marshmallows:** In a large saucepan over low heat, melt butter. Add marshmallows and stir until completely melted.
2. **Mix in Cereal:** Remove from heat and add Rice Krispies, stirring until well coated.
3. **Press into Pan:** Press the mixture into a greased 9x13 inch pan.
4. **Cool:** Let cool completely before cutting into squares.
5. **Serve:** Enjoy your treats!

Stuffed Peppers

Ingredients

- 4 large bell peppers (any color)
- 1 lb ground beef or turkey
- 1 cup cooked rice
- 1 cup diced tomatoes (canned or fresh)
- 1 cup shredded cheese (cheddar or your choice)
- 1 teaspoon Italian seasoning
- Salt and pepper to taste

Instructions

1. **Preheat Oven:** Preheat your oven to 375°F (190°C).
2. **Prepare Peppers:** Cut the tops off the peppers and remove the seeds. Place in a baking dish.
3. **Cook Filling:** In a skillet, brown the ground meat. Drain excess fat, then add rice, tomatoes, Italian seasoning, salt, and pepper. Mix well.
4. **Stuff Peppers:** Fill each pepper with the meat mixture, packing it down slightly. Top with shredded cheese.
5. **Bake:** Cover with foil and bake for 25-30 minutes. Remove foil and bake for an additional 10 minutes until cheese is bubbly.
6. **Serve:** Enjoy hot!

Homemade Pizza Rolls

Ingredients

- 1 package of pizza dough (store-bought or homemade)
- 1 cup marinara sauce
- 2 cups shredded mozzarella cheese
- Toppings of your choice (pepperoni, vegetables, etc.)
- Olive oil for brushing

Instructions

1. **Preheat Oven:** Preheat your oven to 400°F (200°C).
2. **Roll Out Dough:** On a floured surface, roll out the pizza dough into a rectangle.
3. **Add Filling:** Spread marinara sauce over the dough, leaving a border. Sprinkle cheese and desired toppings on top.
4. **Roll and Cut:** Roll the dough tightly into a log and cut into 1-inch pieces.
5. **Bake:** Place on a baking sheet lined with parchment paper, brush with olive oil, and bake for 15-20 minutes until golden.
6. **Serve:** Enjoy warm with extra marinara for dipping!

Savory Muffins

Ingredients

- 1 ½ cups all-purpose flour
- 1 tablespoon baking powder
- ½ teaspoon salt
- 1 cup shredded cheese (cheddar, feta, etc.)
- 1 cup diced vegetables (spinach, bell peppers, onions)
- 1 cup milk
- 1/3 cup vegetable oil
- 1 large egg

Instructions

1. **Preheat Oven:** Preheat your oven to 350°F (175°C).
2. **Mix Dry Ingredients:** In a bowl, combine flour, baking powder, and salt.
3. **Mix Wet Ingredients:** In another bowl, whisk together milk, oil, and egg.
4. **Combine Mixtures:** Pour the wet mixture into the dry ingredients and stir until just combined. Fold in cheese and vegetables.
5. **Fill Muffin Tin:** Pour batter into a greased muffin tin, filling each cup about 2/3 full.
6. **Bake:** Bake for 18-20 minutes until golden and a toothpick comes out clean.
7. **Serve:** Enjoy warm!

Fruit Smoothies

Ingredients

- 2 cups frozen fruit (berries, mango, banana)
- 1 banana (fresh)
- 1 cup yogurt (Greek or regular)
- 1 cup milk or juice
- Optional: honey or maple syrup for sweetness
  Instructions
1. **Blend Ingredients:** In a blender, combine frozen fruit, banana, yogurt, and milk or juice.
2. **Blend Until Smooth:** Blend until creamy and smooth. Add honey if desired.
3. **Serve:** Pour into glasses and enjoy immediately!

Pasta Salad

Ingredients

- 8 oz pasta (rotini, penne, or your choice)
- 1 cup cherry tomatoes, halved
- 1 cucumber, diced
- ½ cup olives (black or green)
- ½ cup Italian dressing
- Salt and pepper to taste
- Optional: feta cheese or mozzarella balls

Instructions

1. **Cook Pasta:** Cook pasta according to package instructions; drain and cool.
2. **Combine Ingredients:** In a large bowl, combine cooked pasta, tomatoes, cucumber, olives, and dressing.
3. **Season:** Add salt and pepper to taste. Stir well to combine.
4. **Chill:** Refrigerate for at least 30 minutes before serving.
5. **Serve:** Enjoy cold or at room temperature!

Baked Zucchini Fries

Ingredients

- 2 medium zucchinis, cut into fries
- ½ cup breadcrumbs
- ¼ cup grated Parmesan cheese
- 1 teaspoon Italian seasoning
- Salt and pepper to taste
- 1 egg, beaten

Instructions

1. **Preheat Oven:** Preheat your oven to 425°F (220°C).
2. **Prepare Coating:** In a bowl, combine breadcrumbs, Parmesan, Italian seasoning, salt, and pepper.
3. **Coat Zucchini:** Dip zucchini fries in the beaten egg, then coat with the breadcrumb mixture.
4. **Arrange on Baking Sheet:** Place on a baking sheet lined with parchment paper in a single layer.
5. **Bake:** Bake for 20-25 minutes, turning halfway, until golden and crispy.
6. **Serve:** Enjoy with your favorite dipping sauce!

S'mores Treats

Ingredients

- 3 tablespoons butter
- 4 cups mini marshmallows
- 6 cups crispy rice cereal
- 1 cup chocolate chips
- ½ cup graham cracker crumbs

Instructions

1. **Melt Butter and Marshmallows:** In a large saucepan, melt butter over low heat. Add marshmallows and stir until completely melted.
2. **Mix in Cereal:** Remove from heat and stir in rice cereal and graham cracker crumbs until well combined.
3. **Add Chocolate Chips:** Fold in chocolate chips gently.
4. **Press into Pan:** Press the mixture into a greased 9x13 inch pan.
5. **Cool:** Let cool completely before cutting into squares.
6. **Serve:** Enjoy your delicious treats!

Chicken Fajitas

Ingredients

- 1 lb chicken breast, sliced
- 1 bell pepper, sliced
- 1 onion, sliced
- 2 tablespoons fajita seasoning
- 2 tablespoons olive oil
- Tortillas for serving
- Optional toppings: sour cream, salsa, cheese, avocado

Instructions

1. **Heat Oil:** In a large skillet, heat olive oil over medium-high heat.
2. **Cook Chicken:** Add sliced chicken and cook until no longer pink, about 5-7 minutes.
3. **Add Vegetables:** Stir in bell pepper, onion, and fajita seasoning. Cook for another 5-7 minutes until vegetables are tender.
4. **Serve:** Serve in warm tortillas with your choice of toppings. Enjoy!

Cucumber Sandwiches

Ingredients

- 1 large cucumber, thinly sliced
- 8 oz cream cheese, softened
- 1 teaspoon dill weed
- 1 teaspoon lemon juice
- 8 slices of bread (white or whole grain)
- Salt and pepper to taste

Instructions

1. **Prepare Cream Cheese:** In a bowl, mix softened cream cheese, dill, lemon juice, salt, and pepper until smooth.
2. **Spread Mixture:** Spread the cream cheese mixture on one side of each slice of bread.
3. **Add Cucumbers:** Layer cucumber slices on half of the bread slices and top with the other slices to form sandwiches.
4. **Cut and Serve:** Cut into quarters or triangles and serve chilled.

Homemade Hummus

Ingredients

- 1 can (15 oz) chickpeas, drained and rinsed
- ¼ cup tahini
- 2 tablespoons olive oil
- 2 tablespoons lemon juice
- 1 clove garlic, minced
- Salt to taste
- Water as needed

Instructions

1. **Blend Ingredients:** In a food processor, combine chickpeas, tahini, olive oil, lemon juice, garlic, and salt.
2. **Adjust Consistency:** Blend until smooth, adding water as needed to reach desired consistency.
3. **Serve:** Transfer to a bowl, drizzle with olive oil, and enjoy with pita or vegetables!

Pasta Primavera

Ingredients

- 8 oz pasta (your choice)
- 2 cups mixed vegetables (bell peppers, zucchini, carrots, broccoli)
- 2 tablespoons olive oil
- 2 cloves garlic, minced
- 1 teaspoon Italian seasoning
- Salt and pepper to taste
- Grated Parmesan cheese for serving

Instructions

1. **Cook Pasta:** Cook pasta according to package instructions; drain and set aside.
2. **Sauté Vegetables:** In a large skillet, heat olive oil over medium heat. Add garlic and mixed vegetables, sautéing until tender, about 5-7 minutes.
3. **Combine:** Add cooked pasta to the skillet, mixing in Italian seasoning, salt, and pepper.
4. **Serve:** Serve warm, topped with grated Parmesan cheese.

Cheese and Crackers Platter

Ingredients

- Assorted cheeses (cheddar, brie, gouda)
- Assorted crackers (water crackers, whole grain, or your choice)
- Optional: grapes, nuts, or dried fruit for garnish

Instructions

1. **Prepare Platter:** Arrange assorted cheeses on a large serving platter.
2. **Add Crackers:** Place crackers around the cheeses.
3. **Garnish:** Add grapes, nuts, or dried fruit for variety.
4. **Serve:** Enjoy as a snack or appetizer!

Mini Meatballs

Ingredients

- 1 lb ground beef or turkey
- 1/2 cup breadcrumbs
- 1/4 cup grated Parmesan cheese
- 1 egg
- 2 cloves garlic, minced
- 1 teaspoon Italian seasoning
- Salt and pepper to taste

Instructions

1. **Preheat Oven:** Preheat your oven to 400°F (200°C).
2. **Mix Ingredients:** In a bowl, combine ground meat, breadcrumbs, Parmesan, egg, garlic, Italian seasoning, salt, and pepper.
3. **Form Meatballs:** Shape mixture into small meatballs (about 1 inch in diameter) and place on a baking sheet.
4. **Bake:** Bake for 15-20 minutes or until cooked through.
5. **Serve:** Enjoy with your favorite sauce or on their own!

Vegetable Soup

Ingredients

- 2 tablespoons olive oil
- 1 onion, diced
- 2 carrots, diced
- 2 celery stalks, diced
- 3 cloves garlic, minced
- 6 cups vegetable broth
- 2 cups mixed vegetables (peas, corn, green beans)
- 1 can (14.5 oz) diced tomatoes
- Salt and pepper to taste
- Optional: fresh herbs for garnish

Instructions

1. **Sauté Vegetables:** In a large pot, heat olive oil over medium heat. Add onion, carrots, and celery, cooking until softened.
2. **Add Garlic:** Stir in garlic and cook for an additional minute.
3. **Add Broth and Vegetables:** Pour in vegetable broth, mixed vegetables, and diced tomatoes. Season with salt and pepper.
4. **Simmer:** Bring to a boil, then reduce heat and simmer for 20-25 minutes.
5. **Serve:** Garnish with fresh herbs if desired and enjoy!

Baked Apple Crisp

Ingredients

- 4 cups sliced apples (about 4 medium apples)
- 1 cup rolled oats
- ½ cup brown sugar
- ½ cup flour
- 1 teaspoon cinnamon
- ½ cup butter, melted

Instructions

1. **Preheat Oven:** Preheat your oven to 350°F (175°C).
2. **Prepare Apples:** Place sliced apples in a greased 9x9 inch baking dish.
3. **Make Topping:** In a bowl, mix oats, brown sugar, flour, cinnamon, and melted butter until crumbly.
4. **Top Apples:** Sprinkle the topping evenly over the apples.
5. **Bake:** Bake for 30-35 minutes, or until apples are tender and topping is golden brown.
6. **Serve:** Enjoy warm, optionally with ice cream!

Peanut Butter Cookies

Ingredients

- 1 cup peanut butter
- 1 cup sugar
- 1 egg
- 1 teaspoon vanilla extract
- ½ teaspoon baking soda

Instructions

1. **Preheat Oven:** Preheat your oven to 350°F (175°C).
2. **Mix Ingredients:** In a bowl, combine peanut butter, sugar, egg, vanilla, and baking soda until smooth.
3. **Shape Cookies:** Roll dough into balls and place on a baking sheet. Flatten with a fork, creating a crisscross pattern.
4. **Bake:** Bake for 10-12 minutes, or until edges are lightly golden.
5. **Serve:** Let cool on the baking sheet before transferring to a wire rack. Enjoy!

Taco Salad

Ingredients

- 1 lb ground beef or turkey
- 1 packet taco seasoning
- 1 head romaine lettuce, chopped
- 1 cup cherry tomatoes, halved
- 1 cup canned black beans, drained and rinsed
- 1 cup corn (canned or frozen)
- 1 cup shredded cheese (cheddar or Mexican blend)
- Tortilla chips for serving
- Optional toppings: salsa, sour cream, avocado

Instructions

1. **Cook Meat:** In a skillet, cook ground meat until browned. Drain excess fat and add taco seasoning according to package instructions.
2. **Prepare Salad:** In a large bowl, combine lettuce, tomatoes, black beans, corn, and cheese.
3. **Assemble:** Add the cooked meat to the salad and toss gently.
4. **Serve:** Serve with tortilla chips and optional toppings. Enjoy!

Chocolate Mug Cake

Ingredients

- 4 tablespoons all-purpose flour
- 4 tablespoons sugar
- 2 tablespoons unsweetened cocoa powder
- 1/8 teaspoon baking powder
- 3 tablespoons milk
- 2 tablespoons vegetable oil
- 1/4 teaspoon vanilla extract
- Optional: chocolate chips for added sweetness

Instructions

1. **Mix Dry Ingredients:** In a microwave-safe mug, combine flour, sugar, cocoa powder, and baking powder.
2. **Add Wet Ingredients:** Stir in milk, vegetable oil, and vanilla extract until smooth. Mix in chocolate chips if using.
3. **Microwave:** Microwave on high for about 1 minute and 30 seconds, or until the cake has risen and is set in the middle.
4. **Serve:** Let cool for a minute before enjoying directly from the mug!

Egg Salad Sandwiches

Ingredients

- 6 hard-boiled eggs, chopped
- 1/4 cup mayonnaise
- 1 teaspoon Dijon mustard
- 1 tablespoon chopped chives or green onions
- Salt and pepper to taste
- Bread for serving (white, whole grain, or your choice)

Instructions

1. **Mix Ingredients:** In a bowl, combine chopped eggs, mayonnaise, mustard, chives, salt, and pepper. Mix well.
2. **Assemble Sandwiches:** Spread egg salad on slices of bread, then top with another slice.
3. **Cut and Serve:** Cut sandwiches into quarters or halves and serve chilled.

Oven-Baked Fish Sticks

Ingredients

- 1 lb white fish fillets (cod, tilapia, etc.)
- 1 cup breadcrumbs
- 1/2 cup flour
- 2 eggs, beaten
- 1 teaspoon paprika
- Salt and pepper to taste
- Optional: lemon wedges for serving

Instructions

1. **Preheat Oven:** Preheat your oven to 425°F (220°C).
2. **Prepare Coating:** Set up three bowls: one with flour, one with beaten eggs, and one with breadcrumbs mixed with paprika, salt, and pepper.
3. **Coat Fish:** Dip each fish piece first in flour, then in the egg, and finally in the breadcrumb mixture, pressing to adhere.
4. **Bake:** Place on a baking sheet lined with parchment paper and bake for 15-20 minutes, or until golden and cooked through.
5. **Serve:** Serve with lemon wedges if desired. Enjoy!

Fruit and Yogurt Cups

Ingredients

- 2 cups yogurt (plain or flavored)
- 2 cups mixed fresh fruit (berries, banana, kiwi, etc.)
- 1/4 cup granola

Instructions

1. **Layer Ingredients:** In cups or bowls, layer yogurt, mixed fruit, and granola.
2. **Repeat Layers:** Repeat layers until cups are filled.
3. **Serve:** Enjoy immediately as a refreshing snack or breakfast!

Zucchini Noodles

Ingredients

- 2 medium zucchinis
- 1 tablespoon olive oil
- 2 cloves garlic, minced
- Salt and pepper to taste
- Optional: grated Parmesan cheese for serving

Instructions

1. **Spiralize Zucchini:** Use a spiralizer to create zucchini noodles (zoodles) or use a vegetable peeler for ribbons.
2. **Sauté:** In a skillet, heat olive oil over medium heat. Add garlic and sauté for 1 minute.
3. **Add Zoodles:** Add zucchini noodles to the skillet and sauté for 2-3 minutes until tender. Season with salt and pepper.
4. **Serve:** Serve warm, topped with grated Parmesan cheese if desired.

Homemade Salsa

Ingredients

- 4 ripe tomatoes, diced
- 1 small onion, diced
- 1 jalapeño, seeded and minced
- 1/4 cup cilantro, chopped
- Juice of 1 lime
- Salt to taste

Instructions

1. **Combine Ingredients:** In a bowl, combine diced tomatoes, onion, jalapeño, cilantro, and lime juice.
2. **Season:** Add salt to taste and mix well.
3. **Serve:** Enjoy with tortilla chips or as a topping for tacos!

Pasta with Pesto

Ingredients

- 8 oz pasta (your choice)
- 1/2 cup pesto (store-bought or homemade)
- 1/4 cup grated Parmesan cheese
- Salt and pepper to taste
- Optional: cherry tomatoes or pine nuts for garnish

Instructions

1. **Cook Pasta:** Cook pasta according to package instructions; drain and reserve some pasta water.
2. **Combine:** In a large bowl, toss hot pasta with pesto, adding a bit of reserved pasta water to help combine if necessary.
3. **Season:** Season with salt and pepper to taste.
4. **Serve:** Serve warm, garnished with grated Parmesan and optional toppings.

Mini Quiches

Ingredients

For the crust:

- 1 package of pre-made pie crusts or phyllo dough (or you can make your own)

For the filling:

- 4 large eggs
- 1 cup milk (or cream for a richer flavor)
- 1 cup shredded cheese (cheddar, mozzarella, or your choice)
- 1 cup diced vegetables (spinach, bell peppers, mushrooms, etc.)
- 1 cup cooked meat (bacon, ham, or sausage) - optional
- Salt and pepper to taste
- Fresh herbs (thyme, parsley, or chives) - optional

Instructions

1. **Preheat the oven:** Preheat your oven to 375°F (190°C).
2. **Prepare the crust:**
   - Roll out the pie crusts and cut them into circles to fit into a muffin tin. Press the circles into the muffin cups to form small cups.
3. **Prepare the filling:**
   - In a mixing bowl, whisk together the eggs and milk. Season with salt and pepper.
   - Stir in the cheese, vegetables, meat (if using), and herbs.
4. **Fill the crusts:**
   - Pour the egg mixture into each crust, filling them about ¾ full.
5. **Bake:**
   - Bake for 20-25 minutes or until the egg is set and the tops are golden brown.
6. **Cool and serve:**
   - Let them cool for a few minutes before removing from the muffin tin. Serve warm or at room temperature.

Tips

- **Customization:** Feel free to mix and match ingredients based on what you have on hand.

- **Storage:** Mini quiches can be stored in the fridge for a few days or frozen for later use.

Enjoy your delicious mini quiches!

Frozen Yogurt Bark

Ingredients

- 2 cups Greek yogurt (plain or flavored)
- 2 tablespoons honey or maple syrup (optional, for sweetness)
- 1 cup mixed toppings (fresh fruit, nuts, granola, chocolate chips, etc.)

Instructions

1. **Prepare the yogurt:**
    - In a bowl, mix the Greek yogurt with honey or maple syrup if you want it sweeter.
2. **Spread the yogurt:**
    - Line a baking sheet with parchment paper. Spread the yogurt evenly on the parchment, about 1/4 to 1/2 inch thick.
3. **Add toppings:**
    - Sprinkle your choice of toppings evenly over the yogurt.
4. **Freeze:**
    - Place the baking sheet in the freezer and freeze for about 4-6 hours, or until the yogurt is completely solid.
5. **Break into pieces:**
    - Once frozen, remove the bark from the baking sheet and break it into pieces.
6. **Store:**
    - Store any leftovers in an airtight container in the freezer.

Tips

- **Fruit:** Use berries, banana slices, or chopped mango for fresh toppings.
- **Customization:** Get creative with toppings like shredded coconut, peanut butter drizzles, or granola for added crunch.
- **Serving:** Enjoy as a refreshing snack or dessert!

Enjoy your frozen yogurt bark!

www.ingramcontent.com/pod-product-compliance
Lightning Source LLC
LaVergne TN
LVHW081330060526
838201LV00055B/2547